AUTISM & YOU

Learning in Styles

Diana Friedlander, EdD
& Karen Burke, EdD

AUTISM & YOU: Learning in Styles

All marketing and publishing rights guaranteed to and reserved by:

721 W. Abram Street
Arlington, TX 76013
(800) 489-0727
(817) 277-0727
(817) 277-2270 (fax)
E-mail: info@fhautism.com
www.fhautism.com

Cover & interior design by John Yacio III
Pencil/arrow art by graphixmania/Depositphotos

ISBN: 978-1-9417654-5-6

Contents

1

So You Have Autism

So you have autism, what exactly does this mean for you? It is a fact that more than 1 in about 68 people in the United States has some form of autism. This means that other kids in your school have autism; baseball players, dancers, musicians, and teachers have autism. People in the grocery store, at the pool, and in the library have autism.

There are many things you can do about yourself; for instance, if you are heavy, you can lose weight or if you are slow at figuring out multiplication problems, you can practice your multiplication facts, or if you are particularly talented in art, perhaps you can take more classes. However, you cannot change the fact that you have autism. What you can do is learn more about autism and begin to understand how it affects you and your life. This book is designed to help you do just that, discover and use your strengths to reach your goals and better understand how you learn. Knowing yourself and speaking up for who you are and what you need is called self-advocacy. This book will give you information about your learning style and your autism so you can make a plan for success. Let's take a look at what the experts have to say about autism.

 ## How It All Began

When you were young, your parents took you to your pediatrician for regular checkups. Most likely, during one of the checkups, your parents and the doctor discussed some of their concerns about your development. Autism is considered a developmental exceptionality, so somewhere along the line, your development was different from that of most kids your age and your brothers and sisters. Maybe you did not start speaking in sentences when most kids do (2 years or so). Maybe it was hard for you to look at people when they talked to you or to join in the large-group activities at preschool and maybe you felt uncomfortable when someone hugged or cuddled you. Does any of this sound familiar? These are just some of the things parents keep an eye on as their children grow. They are often called benchmarks or developmental milestones.

CHAPTER 1: So You Have Autism

When your parents and your doctor began to talk about your development, they began to realize how unique you are. Your parents were probably concerned when they first became aware of your developmental differences. Possibly the doctor talked to them about autism and how people who have autism are sometimes different in some ways than people who do not have autism. A conversation about autism can be tricky because no two people are alike. People who have autism are sometimes said to be "quirky" or different because they do not always see the world like most people do. This is not to say they are wrong, only that they are different. Your parents may not have even heard of autism. They probably had to do some research to better understand what a diagnosis of autism really meant for you and the entire family. In addition to reading what the experts said, they may have talked to other parents of children who had received a similar diagnosis to get advice from them.

They probably also read books written by other parents who have children with autism, books written by someone like Eustacia Cutler, who has a famous daughter with autism, Temple Grandin. Although Temple had a hard time connecting with people and sometimes became very frustrated as a child, she grew up to be a college professor, engineer, and lecturer about autism. She was born in the 1950s when people knew very little about autism—some people even thought she was crazy and wanted her locked away, which is something we would never think or do today. Her mother felt alone and confused when she first learned her daughter had autism. She did not have the support of doctors or friends who understood Temple's differences.

In her book about being Temple's mother, she writes about Temple as a little girl: "Temple is causing storms from which there is no quick tidy-up and no immediate answer. This is a new experience for both of us ...." Neither Temple nor her mother really understood why she was having these behavior problems. Once they both learned more about her autism, they worked together so Temple could find better ways to express herself. She learned that she could talk about her frustrations and set up schedules and reminders so she would not feel so overwhelmed or disoriented about her day. She also figured out ways to get the sensory input she needed to feel calmer (more about that later). Today, she speaks to people all over the world about her experiences as a mother of a child with autism.

Doug Flutie, a famous football player, also has a son who has autism. He and his wife started the Doug Flutie, Jr. Foundation to help people with autism by raising money to support research into what causes autism. He even created and sold cereal called "Fluties" to help raise money for his foundation.

CHAPTER 1: So You Have Autism

When told that you had autism, your parents may have had similar experiences as these parents. They may have been uncertain and confused. They may have turned to the Internet to get information or to books or lectures offered by other parents of children with similar development and behavior patterns. Every family is different. Families are made up of people and each of them is unique. Some families move around a lot, some are skiers, some have red hair, and some have autism. Your family is as unique as all others. Now you are old enough to begin to try to understand yourself and to investigate what it is that makes you you. Everyone has strengths and challenges. You already know that some of yours are quirky or different from other kids your age or from your brothers and sisters. There are times when you just need to be you and cannot muster the interest or energy to figure out how to get things done - times when you might need to curl up inside yourself and take a break or speak out at someone to make your thoughts known. Sometimes those moments can be extra challenging for those who live with you, especially your parents, whose job it is to help mold you to grow up. All kids your age are challenging for parents; they are becoming more independent and do not always feel they need to follow the flow of the family, they keep their rooms messy and do not like to be reminded to do their homework. You can probably see yourself in these examples but your autism often requires even more understanding and patience from your family and more hard work from you. Taking a simple test to help you determine your learning style preferences can give you the tools you need to begin to advocate for yourself. For example, if you discover you learn best while working with others, maybe doing your homework alone in your room is not the best way to get it done or if you work best while snacking, perhaps you can make certain to take an extra snack to math class (of course, after discussing it with your math teacher). Anything you and your parents can do to help all of you understand your autism will make your path to growing up smoother for everyone.

 ## Understanding Autism

Autism has been around for a long time. As early as the 1940s, doctors began to use the term autism when referring to a person who appeared to be very withdrawn. Two doctors in particular were working on the same research, Dr. Asperger in Europe and Dr. Kanner in the United States. However, because of World War II, they never had a chance to meet and exchange ideas, although both had developed a pretty good understanding of autism.

CHAPTER 1: So You Have Autism

In the 1960s, a doctor in the United States named Bruno Bettelheim wrote books about psychology and autism. In his books, he claimed that autism was caused by mothers who acted cold and withdrawn from their babies. You can imagine how Temple Grandin's mother felt when she read this! We have since learned that this is not true and that autism is caused by a person's genetic makeup and environment, not by a mother's behavior.

Science and research in autism has come a long, long way since then. Now doctors have a good idea of why some people are born with autism. They have discovered that autism is caused by a person's genetic makeup. Everyone is made up of cells and inside every cell is something called your DNA. This is a "map" of your genes or genetic makeup. It helps make us individuals. Scientists have also discovered that autism is more likely to occur in boys and that many people have some form of autism. They have learned that autism is a spectrum disorder, which means it can look very different in different people. Think of the autism spectrum as a tape measure or ruler with an infinite number of tiny lines along one edge. One end of that scale would be considered severe autism. If you had severe autism you might not be able to speak or interact with others at all. You might have significant sensory needs that make it difficult for you to even open your eyes or move about. At the other end of the tape measure (spectrum) is someone who has mild autism, which can also be called high-functioning autism spectrum disorder. This can describe someone who has a lot of language but some characteristics of autism, such as being very rigid and finding it difficult to accept change.

You are one of those ticks along that line, which includes an infinite number of lives. Your autism and how it affects your life places you on one of those ticks. Can people move along the spectrum? Absolutely, as you grow and change and begin to understand your autism, the possibilities are endless for you. The more you understand, the better you are able to figure out how to manage things that might have been difficult for you. For example, as a small child, you may not have understood how important it was for you to learn to wait. Waiting was really, really hard for you and you might have pushed ahead of your classmates or sisters and brothers to get somewhere first. Now you have learned that waiting is OK; you have worked on it and know that you will get to your destination and that you are fine being second, fourth, or even last. You've learned how to manage something which was difficult for you in order to grow. It still may feel uncomfortable for you, but you learned to change your behaviors for the better.

How Did You Get to Be Autistic?

As mentioned earlier, your parents might have taken you to a pediatrician when you were a baby. The doctor or your parents noticed that your development and maybe your behavior were different from other children. Children develop at different rates, but your development was considered to be beyond the differences within the range that doctors usually see.

Your parents and doctor discussed your differences in development and decided to give you some tests to get a clearer picture of just what was going on with you. The doctor probably observed your behavior and asked your parents a lot of questions about how you reacted to the world around you, then took this information and looked at it carefully, comparing it to most children your age. And, based on that, the doctor determined that you had autism. Exactly where you fell along the autism spectrum helped the doctor and your parents develop a plan for just what they needed to do. Did you have the type of autism that causes you to be very hyper-sensitive to noise to the point that you do not want to play with other children? Did you like to play with one and only one specific toy in one specific way? Maybe you needed speech therapy or a pre-school designed to meet your special needs where the teachers understood that sometimes you learn things differently and developed plans to help you learn more easily. If you had difficulty playing with friends, the teachers may have developed a behavior plan to reward you for sharing and playing to encourage you to do it more often. If you were especially good at designing and building block designs, they may have made sure to give you extra time to build and explore during center time. When adults forgot schedules, dates, or students' names, did they ask for your help?

Sometimes it is not clear that you have autism until you attend school. School is a place with many, many rules to follow and for some people with autism, this can be tricky. Your teachers may have spoken with your parents, talking about how things at school work and how your teachers can help you learn more easily.

Whatever their decisions, your parents knew they had some work to do and set out to help you to learn in the best way possible.

They had to answer their own questions about your strengths and challenges. They had to do a lot of thinking about words like *handicapped*, *special needs*, *gifted*, and *savant* (which refers to someone who is extraordinarily good at one thing in particular). Just where did your differences fit in? Where on the spectrum did you fall?

Now you are old enough to think about these things and help yourself better understand your autism. Throughout your life, you may hear people referring to you as "having autism," "being autistic," or "being on the spectrum." Learning about autism and becoming aware of your learning style preferences are among the first steps you'll take toward better understanding yourself and how you learn. Labels are just words for different points of view; you need to figure out what they mean for you.

 ## Autism in the Classroom

When a new school year begins, teachers get a list of the names of all the students in their class. Sometimes that's all they get—a list of names. We know that people are a lot more complex than just their names, but sometimes teachers don't get that more detailed information about their students. However, with time and information from you or your parents about just what makes you you, they will figure it out—they are smart people. Teachers can tell pretty early on when someone does not follow the same path as everyone else (think about that example we read of how hard it can be for some people with autism to wait or how upsetting it can be when the daily schedule gets turned upside down when there is a guest author or school-wide performance). What teachers sometimes have difficulty understanding is why school can be so difficult for you and what simple changes might make it easier.

Our schools are designed to teach many students of about the same age at the same time. This means that second-grade teachers have a pretty good idea of what makes a seven-year-old tick, just as a fourth-grade teacher has a good read on nine-year-olds. While many teachers' present material and change the way they teach by screening students for interests or skills, some still teach all students in their class the same thing in the same way.

That's where you and your autism may run into trouble! We have already determined that you are not like everyone else. You sometimes think and react differently, which means your teachers need more information about you. You can help your teacher learn more about your autism by sharing what you learn about your preferred learning style and what that means *for you*. Sometimes all it takes for you to succeed is for everyone to agree that you will have the opportunity to do things a bit differently than your classmates.

Classrooms can be very busy places. Teachers try to make their classrooms as comfortable for students as possible. However, sometimes what is comfortable for other students is not comfortable for you. Say the teacher seats you next to the heating or air conditioning unit. Most kids wouldn't be concerned about this—they probably wouldn't even notice it. But you, because of your autism, may have a keener sense of hearing, so the constant hum of the machinery may keep you from hearing one word the teacher says. When this happens, the teacher is thinking, "That kid is not listening to me." At the same time, you are thinking, "I wish I wasn't sitting here where it is difficult for me to concentrate with that humming going on."

Can you see how helpful it could be for you and your teacher when you share what you have learned about your autism and your preferred learning style? That's called *self-advocacy*. This means understanding what works best for you and working with others to make that happen. It will become a useful tool for you when you learn to use it with respect for yourself as well as others.

Teachers want to be the best teachers possible for all their students, but often they are overwhelmed by the many and different needs in their classrooms. If 25 students are in a class, there are at least 25 differences. All people are individuals; some come to school without solid knowledge of the English language, some might find it difficult to hear the teacher, or some may have difficulty sitting still for more than 10 minutes. Teachers have a tough job with a lot of material to teach to a variety of very different people. The more you can help your teachers learn about your learning style preferences and your autism, the better school will be for you. Ask your teacher if you can meet to discuss what you have learned and together you can brainstorm some strategies.

In the following chapters, you will learn about different ways to learn new information, or your learning style, which way of learning feels most comfortable for you (called *your preferred learning style*), and how to determine these preferences. Once you know what they are, you can use that knowledge to learn and grow.

2

You Also Have a Learning Style

Learning styles refer to the different ways we concentrate, process, internalize, and remember new and difficult information. When we use, rather than ignore, our natural learning styles, we learn more, more quickly, and with less frustration than when we try to use someone else's style. Your classmate might learn new information by reading a book and then discussing it, but you might prefer to hear your teacher talk about the new information before you read the book. Take a look at the diagram below. It will explain, in a visual way, the five general learning style areas we'll be talking about and some things to think about when you consider how you learn best. These learning style areas are called stimuli on the chart. We will now take a closer look at these learning styles.

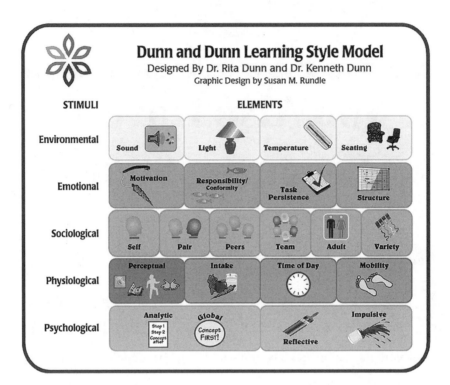

Where You Learn Matters

Learning style strengths are affected by where people prefer to learn. Each one of your classmates may have a different preference for where it is easiest to learn without even knowing it. While concentrating, students react differently to the environment—sound versus silence, bright versus soft lighting, warm versus cool temperatures, and formal versus informal seating.

You can ask your teacher to help you decide what learning space best complements your environmental learning style preferences. For example, you might work best in a more formal space with desks, chairs, and tables. This might be the way your classroom is already designed. Other students may choose informal areas, such as couches, rugs, and soft chairs. Other things to consider include sound preferences, lighting, and temperature. Sometimes simple changes can make a huge difference.

How You Feel About Your Learning Matters

Some students enjoy learning new and difficult material; it makes them feel accomplished! Others strive for good grades because they want their teachers', parents', or friends' approval. When students are interested in what they are learning, they are more motivated to learn. Understanding some of your emotions will help you understand your learning style preferences.

Persistence might mean that you want to stay with one task until it is finished or work on multiple tasks at the same time. Some students feel a need to complete one task before beginning another. They rarely feel the need to take breaks while learning. Other students prefer to take breaks while they learn. Still others prefer to work on multiple tasks at the same time. *Responsibility* is another emotion related to the emotional needs of your learning style. It is most related to times when you must do what others have told you to do. Students who enjoy doing the opposite of what most people do are called *nonconformists*. This is where you can run into big trouble. If you and the adults who help you can begin to understand this about you, they might try having discussions with you, which include being *(a)* spoken to in a respectful manner, *(b)* answering your many "why" questions and *(c)* giving you lots of choices of how to complete an assignment. Remember, it's all about both you and your teacher understanding what works best to help you learn.

Learners also differ in their need for structure. Some want a great deal of direction and feel best when they know what is required and how to proceed. Clear, detailed directions and models to follow can help you here. Students who prefer less structure enjoy doing things their way. Once you become aware of what's best for you, your teacher and you can brainstorm different paths to get to the same goal.

People You Choose to Learn with Matters

You might prefer to learn alone, in groups, along with an adult, and/or in a variety of ways instead of routine patterns. To learn, some students require interaction and discussion, so for them learning in small groups where they can bounce ideas off each other is important. For others, a whole-class lesson works just fine. You and your teacher might discuss what makes you more comfortable in the classroom, motivating you to learn more easily. For example, a simple change in who you work with can have a big effect on what you learn.

How Your Body Feels While You Are Learning Matters

Your physical body also influences how you learn and is a part of your learning style. Sometimes you are affected by how you take things into your brain. How you do this can be called your perceptual strengths, like what and how you are hearing (auditory), what you see and how (visual), whether or not you need to handle or feel materials (tactual), and your desire to move about while learning (kinesthetic). While most younger students are more tactual and kinesthetic, the older you become, the more likely you are to prefer learning in an auditory or visual way. Remember, that's for most students, but not necessarily you.

Physiological preferences also include time of day and need for snacks and movement breaks. Some students concentrate better in the early or late morning, while others do not focus well until afternoon; some are low-energy all day and first become energetic at night. Some students need to move about from one part of the classroom to another or they will lose a lot of their ability to think; others do not need to move about at all. Some students learn more when they are eating or drinking; others can only nibble or snack when they relax after studying.

Most teachers expect students to sit still and pay attention. You will need to talk with your teachers about helping you create ways to learn in the way that is best for you without being disruptive to the rest of the kids in the room.

How You Understand Information Matters

Analytic thinkers begin to work in a step-by-step sequence. They keep at a task until they have learned what they need or want to or accomplished what they set out to do. *Global thinkers* initially process information by thinking of everything related to what they need or want to learn. They may take many breaks, but eventually they focus on the most important information and complete the task. Both types of processing—analytic and global—are good, but students who have one style versus the other learn very differently from each other. Analytics prefer to concentrate on a series of facts that move toward a gradual understanding of an over-all concept. Having information introduced in a step-by-step approach enables children with analytic styles to learn best. Global learners need to understand concepts before they start concentrating on details. Endless facts tend to bore them and they lose interest fast. They understand things better when they are introduced to them through short stories, illustrations, humor, or anecdotes. Globals like to learn by being actively involved with information that is interesting and related to their lives.

After reading this book, you will understand that everyone has strengths but that each person's strengths are different. Learning styles are based on reactions to many different things in your life, including feelings, routines, and events. The next chapter will give you information about an online learning style assessment test. This test will help you learn about your strengths after you honestly answer a series of questions that will not be graded. There are no wrong answers! Your honest answers will give you information that will make it easier for you to learn.

3

Discovering Your Learning Style:
Taking a Test You Can't Fail

Your learning style is based on your reactions to different triggers, feelings, and patterns that feel comfortable to you while you are learning. Those patterns tend to be most appreciated when you concentrate on new or difficult material. Regardless of your learning style and the strategies used, your individual learning style will enable you to learn and realize nothing is wrong with others who learn in a different style; rather, everyone learns differently. You will observe that you can demonstrate increased levels of patience knowing that, though one activity wasn't your preferred way of working, it was appropriate for a classmate.

Your learning style is made up of several parts. There are at least 21 different variables (or parts) to consider, including environmental, emotional, sociological, physiological, and psychological references, which we just discussed. It is not possible to identify all the elements of your learning style pattern just through observation. Some elements of style cannot be seen even by the experienced eye of a teacher or parent and the behaviors associated with other elements can be misinterpreted. Therefore, it is important to identify your learning style with a test that many people have taken and that is guaranteed to measure what we need it to measure. Research studies have proven that it is possible to correctly identify learning style preferences.

 ## What Does the LS:CY! Assessment Test Do?

School classrooms, families, and various cultures have different styles. Your mother's style is likely to be different from your father's style and their styles are probably different from your friends' and classmates' styles.

Everyone has strengths, but each person's strengths are different. Learning styles are based on complex reactions to many different things in your life, including feelings, routines, and events. As a result, patterns often develop and repeat whenever anyone concentrates on new and difficult material.

The best way to learn about your strengths is by honestly answering a series of questions that will be analyzed, not graded. Only honest answers result in information that makes it easier for you to learn. Do not give the answer that you think your teacher or parents want you to give. Be honest!

 ## Discovering Your Learning Style

Using the LS:CY! Test

You can go to www.learningstyles.net and read more information about learning styles and the LS:CY; you can even view demonstration videos. Talk with your parents about how knowing more about your learning style will make it easier for you to learn. Here is an overview of a really helpful learning style assessment tool. It will help you identify how you prefer to learn.

- Gives you a computerized picture of your preferred learning style, called the *One Page Student Report.*

- Gives you suggestions for redesigning your learning environment based on your need for sound, quiet, bright or soft light, temperature, or seating.

- Indicates the methods and materials through which you are likely to do your best work.

- Pinpoints the best time during the day for you to be involved in required difficult subjects.

- Tells you if snacks and drinks while learning may help you.

- Notes if you are the type of student for whom movement while learning may facilitate the learning process.

- Suggests which analytic or global approaches to learning new and difficult material are likely to be important for you.

The LS:CY! Considers Individual Preferences in the Following Areas

- *Environmental:* sound, light, temperature, and seating

- *Emotionality:* motivation, persistence, responsibility/conformity and need for structure

- *Sociological factors:* learning alone, with a partner, as part of a small group or team, with peers, with an adult, and/or in a combination of ways

- *Physiological factors:* auditory, visual, tactual, and/or kinesthetic perceptual preferences; food or liquid intake, time-of-day energy levels, and mobility needs

- *Psychological factors:* global or analytic learner? Five stories are presented using fantasy, imagery, humor, and pictures. Each of the five stories refers to students solving a mystery by using three areas of learning style elements. The stories all contain the theme of mystery and detectives. Each story is followed by a series of 69 questions about your individual learning style.

The titles of the stories are:

1. The Case of the Shattering Windows
2. The Case of the Wrong Directions
3. The Case of the Unwelcome Bat
4. The Case of the Mummy's Ring
5. The Case of the Strange Noise

Each question is repeated three times throughout the test. You will respond to each question using a multiple-choice format. Each possible response includes a picture image that is representative of the answer.

It is not necessary to read every story, unless you want to. Once you understand what is required after reading the first or second story, you

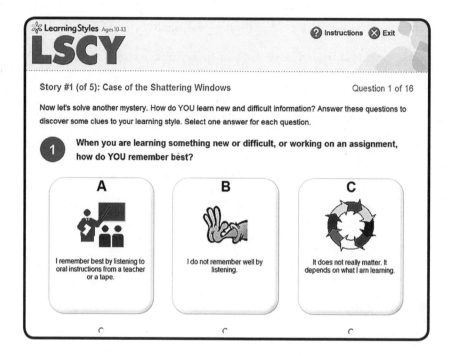

need only answer the questions at the end of each of the five stories. It is important to remember that there are no right or wrong answers! Just choose the answer that you feel best describes you.

You can complete the test alone, with friends, in a classroom, at home, or in a computer lab. You can read the stories and questions by yourself or an adult or another student can read them to you. The test should take no longer than 40 minutes to complete, but it is not necessary to finish in one time period. If you wish, you can stop after any one of the five stories and log on later to complete the assessment.

The Results

After completing the test, you receive a short, one-page report of your learning style preferences and a full report. The sample below is a one-page student report. It shows a student's preference or strong preference for each learning style element. Look for the white dot on each line to help you understand where this student's learning style preference lies along the path from, say, "dim" to "bright" light. You can easily see that he prefers to work in dim light. Dots that fall near the middle suggest the student doesn't feel very strongly one way or the other about this particular element.

Student:	Tom Styles	Grade:	6
Group/Class:	Class of 2017	Age:	11
Completed:	06/19/2014	Gender:	Male

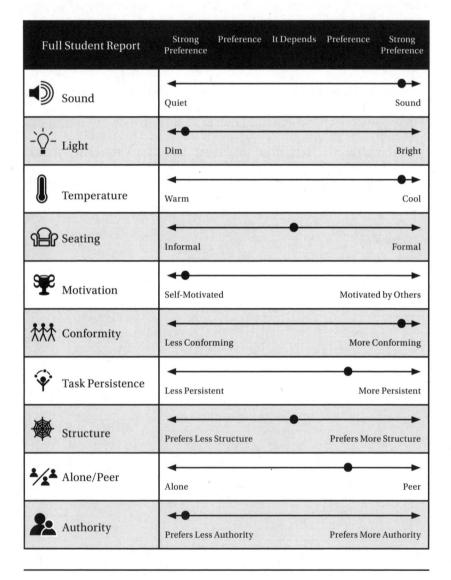

Full Student Report	Strong Preference	Preference	It Depends	Preference	Strong Preference
Variety	Prefers Less Authority				Prefers More Authority
Auditory	Does Not Learn Best by Listening			Learn by Listening	
Visual	Does Not Learn Best by Seeing				Learns by Seeing
Kinesthetic	Does Not Learn Best by Moving				Learns by Moving
Tactile	Does Not Learn Best by Touching				Learns by Touching
Intake	Does Not Need Intake		Needs Intake		
Morning/Evening	Prefers Morning				Prefers Evening
Late Morning	Does Not Prefer Late Morning				Prefers Late Morning
Afternoon	Does Not Prefer Afternoon				Prefers Afternoon
Mobility	Stationary				Movement
Reflective/ Impulsive	Reflective				Impulsive
Analytic/ Global	Analytic		Integrated		Global

The full report is designed to give you, your parents, and teachers examples of how to best use your learning style strengths. Here is an example.

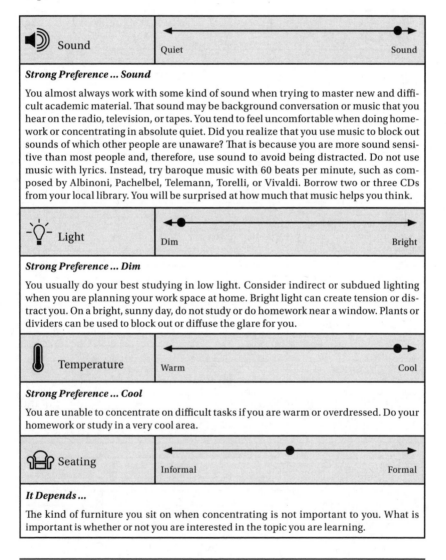

Strong Preference ... Sound

You almost always work with some kind of sound when trying to master new and difficult academic material. That sound may be background conversation or music that you hear on the radio, television, or tapes. You tend to feel uncomfortable when doing homework or concentrating in absolute quiet. Did you realize that you use music to block out sounds of which other people are unaware? That is because you are more sound sensitive than most people and, therefore, use sound to avoid being distracted. Do not use music with lyrics. Instead, try baroque music with 60 beats per minute, such as composed by Albinoni, Pachelbel, Telemann, Torelli, or Vivaldi. Borrow two or three CDs from your local library. You will be surprised at how much that music helps you think.

Strong Preference ... Dim

You usually do your best studying in low light. Consider indirect or subdued lighting when you are planning your work space at home. Bright light can create tension or distract you. On a bright, sunny day, do not study or do homework near a window. Plants or dividers can be used to block out or diffuse the glare for you.

Strong Preference ... Cool

You are unable to concentrate on difficult tasks if you are warm or overdressed. Do your homework or study in a very cool area.

It Depends ...

The kind of furniture you sit on when concentrating is not important to you. What is important is whether or not you are interested in the topic you are learning.

The printed reports that are generated on the LS:CY! website are very helpful for describing learning style preferences to you, your parents, and your teachers. It is important to spend time with your teachers and parents discussing your learning style preferences, how your preferences differ from those of your friends, and how you can best use your preferences to learn more efficiently.

 ## Understanding Learning Styles

After examining your profile, you might want to predict the styles of your family members by describing behaviors that suggest characteristics representative of learning styles. Ask your relatives and see how accurately they guess. You might even want to write poems or stories or draw pictures about how you feel about the results of your LS:CY.

Once you understand your profile, you will need to investigate it further. For instance, if you discover that you are a tactual or kinesthetic learner, you may want to learn how to teach yourself using tactual and kinesthetic methods. Chapter Five provides step-by-step instructions to develop your own Electroboards, Flip Chutes, Pic-A-Holes, Task Cards, and other resource strategies that teach tactual learners to absorb difficult information through their perceptual strength.

Meanwhile, discuss the results of the learning style assessment with your parents and teachers. They will understand what the learning style guidelines mean and how to use them. You can work together to begin using your preferred learning styles.

4

Where?
Strategies to Help You Feel More Comfortable While You Are Learning

Learning style strengths and weaknesses are affected by where people learn. Look around your classroom; each one of your classmates may have a different preference for where it is easiest to learn. While concentrating, students react differently to the environment—sound versus silence, bright versus soft lighting, warm versus cool temperatures, and formal versus informal seating.

You and your teacher can best decide how to evaluate your classroom so that you will be learning in a space that complements your environmental learning style preferences. By making simple changes in the classroom and your work space at home, you can create space to work in formal/structured areas which might include desks, chairs, and tables or informal/less structured areas sometimes made up of couches, rugs, and soft chairs. You will also need to consider sound preferences, lighting needs, and temperature controls, depending on how they make you feel while you are learning. Sometimes simple changes can make a huge difference. When your body feels comfortable and safe, your brain can concentrate on learning.

 ## Sound vs. Silence

When you think about your learning environment, you have to consider several things. One is the level of sound in the room. Noise in the environment makes some people anxious and overwhelmed. Are you the type of person who prefers not to go to a movie theater because the sound is often turned up so high? If so, you have probably figured out that renting movies and watching them in your own quiet space works much better for you, and you still get to enjoy the movie. Some people prefer to learn in an absolutely quiet environment. They feel that they lose concentration if there is any background noise in the room. Most classrooms are busy places with all kinds of noises. If you are bothered by sound, perhaps you can ask your teacher if you can wear noise-reducing earphones, change your seat to a quiet corner of the room, or use a cardboard study carrel during tasks where you need to concentrate closely.

Others say some kinds of background noise calm them and help them to focus. In fact, experts have found that music can reduce stress and encourage creativity. Often people choose soothing classical music or even music with lyrics, but that is an individual choice. Maybe rock or rap music does it for you. Have you ever heard of a "white noise" machine? It produces everyday environmental sounds like the sounds of a gentle breeze rustling the trees or ocean waves on the shore. Sometimes such sounds can break up the quiet of a room and help people focus more on the task at hand. Could that work for you?

Once a famous person diagnosed with autism was giving a lecture from a stage in a large auditorium. She was having difficulty staying focused while giving her speech. Finally, she stopped mid-sentence and told everyone that the sound of plates being cleared in the kitchen behind the auditorium was throwing her off track and made it impossible for her to go on. No one in the audience heard the sound of the dishes, but the presenter did, and it kept her from doing her job. Once she made it known that she was having difficulty, the problem was fixed—somebody went back stage and asked the staff to work quietly—and she was able to continue. Knowing what works best for you is key to your success.

Bright Light vs. Soft Light

Another environmental consideration is lighting. Bright overhead lights can feel harsh and over-stimulating to some, whereas a duller, softer light may be too calming and cause others to lose focus or even get sleepy.

Your learning style profile will help you decide what type of lighting helps you concentrate and learn best. Most school classrooms have overhead fluorescent light fixtures, but some schools offer alternative lighting. If your classroom is brightly lit and you feel uneasy with harsh, bright light, talk to someone about this and, with some help from the adults in your life, you may be able to make some simple changes to raise your level of comfort and concentration. Sometimes a simple tool like a colored plastic overlay sheet placed on top of your page changes and softens the look of your work enough to make it more pleasant to read. You can choose from many different colors, finding the one that works best for you. When something is easier to read, your brain tends to understand it better. Sometimes moving your seat closer to a window, a natural light source, gives you just the softness you need while the overhead lights allow you to see your work clearly. As school administrators become more aware of lighting preferences, libraries, study halls, and other common rooms are being outfitted with reading lamps and are not lit solely by overhead fixtures. Lamps like this create a softer and gentler light. If bright light works better for you, some simple changes to your learning environment may help. You might find that a bright overlay, say neon yellow, makes words "pop" for you, making them easier to understand. Moving your desk directly under an overhead light or maybe adding a bright desk lamp, spotlighting your work area, may help you with learning without disturbing those around you.

 ## Warm vs. Cool Temperatures

Everyone's body regulates its temperature in a different way. What seems cold to one person may be just right for another. As a result, adjusting the temperature in a classroom so everybody is comfortable can be difficult. Sometimes there is a central thermostat for an entire building that cannot be easily regulated by individual rooms. Here is where you have to plan ahead. If you prefer a cool learning environment, dress cool. Wear layers of clothing that you can easily remove in the classroom, like a sweatshirt or sweater. On the other hand, if you prefer to learn in a snug, toasty environment, add layers until you feel comfortable.

You may know from past experience that clothing can be a major comfort factor or anxiety producer in your life. Some people are highly sensitive to tight or binding clothing. If you are one of these people, you probably feel more comfortable in looser clothing like sweat pants and looser tops; you can learn to avoid distractions, for example, socks and snug shoes that might distract you, with some careful thought. On the flip side, others might seek that nice secure "hug" that you can only get from Under Armor® or Spanx.® Some people say that feeling a slight weight or pressure from their clothing helps them feel calm and collected. If this applies to you, perhaps you can drape a neck support pillow around your shoulders or across your lap during work time to help you feel more grounded. Support pillows are filled with sand, rice, or other weighty materials and can add that bit of pressure. Some are categorized as aroma therapy pillows because they are scented with lavender, vanilla, or other scents. Your sense of smell is one of your most powerful senses. Different scents have a tendency to either calm or alert our bodies. Scents can involve very individualized decisions, so take note. When you are choosing a pillow, make sure that, if it is scented, the scent is right for you or it can be more annoying than helpful. If you feel you need to heighten your arousal, chose a scent that raises your level of alertness; if you feel too "pumped up," a calming scent may be in order. You can do some research in this area to better understand your preferences.

People with autism seem to be more sensitive than most people to what their bodies need to feel comfortable. Draw from your experience in addition to trying new things to help create a learning space where you will do your best.

 ## Formal Seating vs. Informal Seating

Most classrooms are made up of either rows or clusters of desks or communal tables that can seat several students. When thinking about how you are most comfortable learning, think about how you and your teacher can take an educated look at your classroom and brainstorm ways you might rearrange things, sometimes without making huge changes. Maybe you can remain seated in your cluster for most of the day but when it's time for a subject that requires more of your intense concentration you can have access to a clip board and a bean bag chair or soft chair where you know you will be able to feel more comfortable.

While working independently on something, perhaps a small, quiet space like a cubby or "nook" could be set up for you to work uninterrupted for a period of time. If you and the adults helping you take a look around, you will probably find many areas and items already in your classroom that can be used to create small work places. Sometimes it can be as simple as a propped-up file folder, a cut-out cardboard box, or a study carrel. Moving your desk to a quiet corner would create a two-sided space for you to work without distraction. Book cases, desks, filing cabinets, easels, moveable cubbies, and many other classroom fixtures can serve as creative walls and boundaries, helping to build the space that is just right for you. The important point here is that once you learn what works best for you, you can help plan a better work environment for yourself.

The type of chair or seating that you prefer should also be considered. Most student chairs are made of either wood or hard, heavy plastic. They are built to last through many, many students and are not necessarily designed for student comfort. Most kids are fine with this, but you may find this type of seating intolerable. For some, it feels better to replace a typical classroom chair with a big exercise ball. The quiet energy that it takes to hold yourself upright on the ball may also work to increase your focus.

On the other hand, some people prefer to learn in a structured, upright manner. This helps heighten their attention and keeps them interested and focused. You are the only person who knows how your classroom feels to you. Architects, designers, and school personnel try their best to create schools where kids are comfortable learning. Since we already know that sometimes students who have autism learn differently and feel differently from other students, it makes sense that you do not always feel as comfortable as your neighbor. Until now, you may only have been aware of this because of an increased level of stress or anxiety or feeling uninterested and unengaged. Once you have more information about your environmental learning style preference, you will need to give it some thought, discuss it with your parents or teacher, and see if some simple changes can be made to help you. Small adjustments to your environment sometimes make a big difference in terms of the length of time you are able to concentrate on a task as well as how successful you will be.

5

What?
Strategies for Using Hands-On Learning

Tactile Learners Take Notice!

If you frequently tap your fingers, play with objects, wiggle, rock back and forth, get out of your seat, or move your feet, you may be a tactual and/or a kinesthetic. You usually have too much energy to sit still. It helps you to have something to do while concentrating. Your teachers or therapists may have talked to you about "calming your central nervous system" as people with autism sometimes have a greater need to "calm" than others.

Computers can be great learning tools, offering many different ways to learn. For example, games and learning activities can allow you to trace and record the information you read, instantly give you a picture of a word, or even read to you. You can even download apps and websites that help you develop games and puzzles if they are helpful in your learning.

However, while computers or iPads are great for getting information and practicing what you need to learn, they don't always provide enough hands-on feedback for tactile learners. Just swiping a screen, tapping a word, or even tracing may not give you the tactual feedback you need. You might need to actually feel and manipulate the things you work on, such as a cardboard puzzle piece or a flip chart.

This chapter will teach you how to create materials that can help you learn. Some seem very simple, even old-fashioned. They may be simple, but they do the job well. Making, moving, having the opportunity to play with the materials you need to learn is sometimes just the thing to get the information to stick with you.

Students who don't do well in school often have tactile strengths, but are typically asked to learn by listening or reading. When these learners create their own learning materials, Task Cards, Flip Chutes, Pic-A-Holes, and Electroboards, their long-term memory kicks in and they remember what they seek to learn.

Materials and Directions for Making Tactile Materials

Here is a list of all of the materials you need to make tactual resources; just follow the directions to try them. Be sure to share these resources with your parents and teachers when you are finished. Remember what worked for you—use it again and again with different information.

Manipulative Resources

- Flip Chute
- Electroboard
- Task Cards (set)
- Pic-A-Hole
- Learning Circle
- Fact Wheel
- Fact Fan
- Magic Window
- Window Game
- Wrap Around

Materials Needed

- 20 index cards (5"x8")
- 14 paper fasteners
- 2 sheets of tag board (9"x12") or a file folder
- 15" of aluminum foil
- 1 pocket folder
- 1 golf tee
- 1" of Velcro®
- 1 milk or juice carton (half gallon)
- 15" piece of Contact® paper
- a continuity tester;

see www.homedepot.com/p/ Gardner-Bender-Continuity-Tester-GCT-3304/202867880

- 8 clothespins

- 4 paper fasteners

- 8 sheets of tag board (9"x12")

- 24" string of yarn

Supplies

- hole puncher

- ruler

- scissors

- x-acto knife

- washable markers

- masking tape (1 inch width)

Task Cards

- Cut out a set of cards in the same shape or use large index cards.

- Randomly divide each shape into three parts.

- On one part of the shape, print a question. On another part of the shape, print the corresponding answer. Add a picture to the third part.

- Add self-correcting codes through color, picture, shapes, or symbols on the back of each section of the divided shape.

Electroboards

These are pretty cool. You will actually learn how to create an electric circuit that will let you know when you get the answer correct.

- List questions on the left side of a file folder with the answers, out of sequence, on the right side.

- Place one brad on the left side of the file folder for each question. Then place corresponding brads on the right side for the answers.

- Open the file folder and create circuits by connecting a foil strip from each question to the corresponding answer. Be sure the brads are covered with the foil.

- Cover each piece of foil with masking tape before adding the next piece of foil.

- Use a continuity tester to check every circuit to be sure that it is working.

- Close the file folder and seal the edges with tape.

Pic-A-Hole

- Use a pocket folder to create a Pic-A-Hole.

- Cut out the shaded areas, as shown in the diagram.

- Punch out three equally spaced holes below the smaller box.

- Place an index card (5" X 8") in the pocket. Trace the openings onto the card. Remove the traced area from the index card. This will serve as a guide for the placement of questions and answers, which can be written on 5" x 8" index cards.

- Using the 5"x8" index cards, write questions in the appropriate place. Write answers in the space at the bottom. Punch a hole below each answer. Cut a slit for the correct answer.

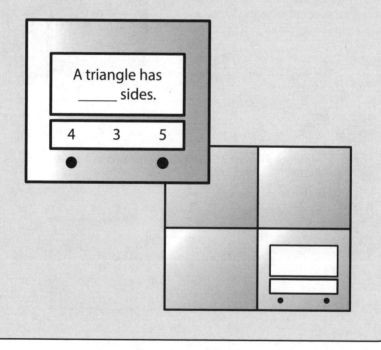

Flip Chute

- Pull open the top of a half-gallon container.

- Remove a 1" strip, 1 ½" from the top.

- Remove a 1" strip, 1 ½"from the bottom.

- Cut 2 index cards; one to measure 6 ½"X 3 ½', the other 7 ½" X 3 ½."

- Attach the smaller strip to the inner openings.

- Attach one side of the larger strip to the bottom opening, the other to the top of the opposite side.

- Make 2" X 2 ½" cards with questions on one side and answers on the other.

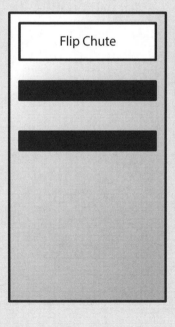

Fact Wheel

- Cut a circle with a diameter of 8" from a piece of tag board. Draw a circle with a diameter of 6" in the center.

- Divide the border into eight sections.

- Write a question in each section of the border. Punch a hole in the center of the circle.

- On another sheet of tag board, draw and cut out a second circle with a diameter of 6". Place an arrow near the edge of the circle.

- To make an answer flap, mark a fold line 45 degrees from the arrow. Cut a flap in the circle. Punch a hole in the center.

- Using a paper fastener, attach the two circles. Turn the arrow to each question around the border, open the flap, and write the answer on the large circle.

Wrap Around

- Start with a sturdy board that is large enough to hold two columns of items. Draw a 1" margin on the left and right.

- Place a column of questions on the left and a column of answers on the right. Place items randomly in each column.

- Cut triangular notches on each side of the board that correspond to the items.

- Punch a hole in the top of the board. Tie a long string in the hole.

- Wrap the string around the back of the board and across to the corresponding answer. Continue to the end.

- Draw a pattern of corresponding lines on the back panel so you can check your answers.

Magic Window

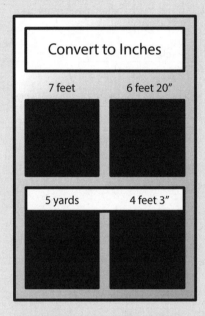

Convert to Inches

7 feet   6 feet 20″

5 yards   4 feet 3″

- Create a pattern of boxes on a piece of tagboard.

- Cut out each box to create a window.

- Write a question or problem above each window. Place a piece of paper under the windows and write the correct answers in the boxes on the paper.

- Flip the tag board over and write the correct answers on the tag board above each window.

- Place the tag board over your paper, insert the answers in each window, and then flip the tag board over to self-correct.

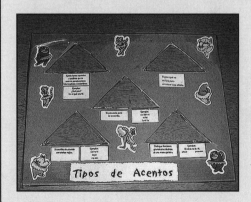

Window Game

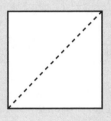

- Fold a square sheet of tagboard in half on a diagonal.

- Unfold the triangle. In the top half of the shape, draw a square for each of your questions.

- Cut each square on three sides. This will create a flap.

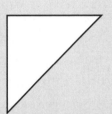

- Fold and glue the two shapes together. Do not glue the flaps.

- Print questions on the front of each flap.

- Fold the flap back and write in the correct answer.

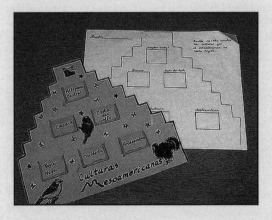

Fact Fan

- Draw a semi-circle with a diameter of 10" on a piece of tagboard. Divide the semi-circle into five or six equal sections.

- Cut the sections into five or six wedges. Make a hole in the point of each wedge.

- Draw a second semi-circle with a diameter of 8". Divide the semi-circle into five or six equal sections. Punch a hole ½" from the bottom of the center.

- Insert a paper fastener into the hole and attach the wedges to the back of the fastener.

- Print questions on each section of the semi-circle. Print answers on the visible edges of the wedges.

- Put a self-correcting symbol on the back of the semi-circle and the same symbol on the corresponding wedge.

Learning Circle

- Cut out a large circle (at least 8″) from oak tag or heavy construction paper.

- Divide the circle into eight equal segments.

- Write a question or problem in each segment.

- Write the answer to each question on the end of a clothespin.

- Color-code or picture-code each correct answer to match its problem. The code should be placed on the back of the circle and the clothespin.

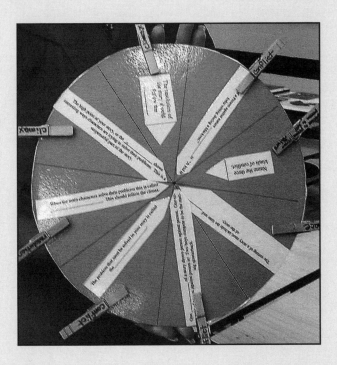

6

How?
Strategies for Understanding Ways You Learn Best

There are two general categories of learners, those who prefer to learn in an analytical manner, which means learning the pieces and then putting them together into a big picture, and global learners, who prefer to start with the big picture and take it apart piece by piece. For instance, some history students think of World War II as one large event with a series of battles and a specific outcome. They view things as "big picture" events. Other students view the war as a series of specific events that favored one side at times and the other side at other times. The parts of the whole stand out most to these students: the battle places, individual victories, or maybe the soldiers themselves. Neither way of learning is better. However, by understanding your learning style, you may understand why you find yourself, for example, reading but not understanding.

Your learning style profile will help you determine which type of learner you are. This can be very important because it gives you an edge in knowing how to attack new and difficult information. People can learn in either way, but feel more comfortable using one or the other, making it easier to learn.

Understanding Analytical Learning: Step-by-Step Learning

The word "analytical" comes from the word "analyze," which means to examine something in great detail to understand it better. Breaking things down into smaller parts may be a helpful way for you to examine things. For instance, let's take a new route to Grandma's house. Analytical learners may want to know each street, the length of time spent traveling, and even alternative ways to go if they meet with traffic or detours. On the other hand, more global learners might want to look at a map of the area to get a general sense of where Grandma lives in relation to themselves and their surroundings.

Teachers tend to present material in an analytical way, giving you the pieces and the tools to help you put them together and learn new material. For example, you are taught that before you write an essay you should map out your plan. This can be done using a graphic organizer or a diagram of each piece or idea, which will come together in the end to be your essay. This method is very helpful to some people, but others don't understand how they can plan something in advance and, therefore, feel more comfortable writing down their thoughts and then going back to edit and revise their work. You can still use a graphic organizer by writing down your big ideas before you begin to write. You can approach the same task in different ways and still end up with a great product.

Analytical learners often prefer to work alone. They have a plan, know where they are going, and sometimes get distracted when working in a group or team. While we all need to learn to work together sometimes, if you prefer to learn new and difficult information on your own, this is something you'll need to discuss with your teacher. If group work is a must, maybe your group can be limited to just one other person or you could meet with your group for a short time and then break apart so each of you can work individually. There are many ways to approach group work.

Analytical learners like systems and plans. They feel a strong need to organize their thinking and approach and then follow through on it. "Going with the flow" or "winging it" makes them feel nervous or unsettled. They are not usually risk takers or experimenters; they question, do their research, develop their plan, and then carry it out step by step. They tend to be critical thinkers who are rational and organized. Learners with analytical strengths are interested in details and facts. They feel more comfortable concentrating on one thing at a time and are not easily distracted while working. Teacher grades, rubrics, and feedback are important to these learners. They like to know what's ahead as they go into a project and feel better attaching their thinking and efforts to the end product. Outlines, notes, organizers, sticky notes, folders, and rubrics are helpful in guiding and planning. These thinkers like to have tangible, organized, materials.

Here are some characteristics of the analytical learner:

- Prefers to study alone for long periods without interruption
- Tends to work on one task to completion
- Focuses on the parts that make up the big picture
- Likely to respond to a problem with logic first, instead of emotion, solves problem systematically and logically

Understanding Global Learning: Looking at the Whole Picture before Breaking It Down

Global learners approach information in a very different way. They look at the big picture. They need to understand a whole idea, often evaluating the overall problem on a large scale before tackling its parts. Sometimes global thinkers are impulsive, skipping the details and plunging right into the problem, not reading the directions, but getting a sense of what needs to be done and getting started on it. These learners need to understand why they are being asked to do something and the purpose of their efforts and, therefore, ask questions to help them understand that big picture. They often prefer to work in small groups, bouncing ideas and information off others, and sharing their ideas and thinking. They enjoy hearing stories and personal narratives about how others have reached their answers.

Here are some characteristics of the global learner:

- May work better in groups than alone

- Prefers to work on multiple tasks at once

- Sees the big picture or overall view

- Likely to respond to a problem with emotion first, instead of logic

More global learners, on the other hand, like to bounce their ideas off others. Discussion about big ideas and overall views may help them better understand the parts of an idea. Sometimes global learners can get a new and different perspective by listening and sharing with their classmates or they just need to talk through an idea to see its strengths and weaknesses.

If you are a global learner, you probably have the ability to understand what is meant by something that is not written explicitly or openly.

You take leaps and risks in your thinking, seeing relationships between information gathered from one place and another. You are not a list maker or a note taker; you prefer to summarize your information and draw on your own experience or that of others. Sometimes global learners like to work on more than one project or task at a time. You can take breaks, put something aside, have a snack, take a walk, work on something else, and come back to a project later after you have given it some thought and pick up right where you left off.

You can think of the terms "global learner" and "analytical learner" as overall labels for deciding which way you typically approach new and difficult information. Both are effective ways of learning and problem solving. Neither is better than the other; each of us has a preferred way of learning.

CHAPTER 6: How?

As you read this chapter, did you have moments when you clearly felt uncomfortable, when your inner voice said, "Oh, no! I would never do that" or when you thought, "Yes, that feels like what I do when I am learning"? People do not generally fit snuggly and securely into either the global or analytical camp. There are situations when you may draw more heavily from one or the other and sometimes from both, but you can see from what you have learned that listening to your inner voice and understanding your comfort level are critical to doing your best and feeling successful. This is just one more piece in discovering who you are as a learner. Knowing how you prefer to learn makes the journey easier and more fun.

7

Who? When?
Understanding with Whom You Learn Best and Managing Your Time

Many students learn best in a mixture of patterns—sometimes alone and sometimes with a partner, in a small group of peers, in a team, or with the teacher. These are called your sociological patterns and may vary with age and achievement. Some people learn consistently in one way, others in varied patterns, and still others have no preference.

However, more global students than analytic students are peer-oriented. These students often learn best with either a single friend or in a small group, in contrast to 13% of all students who learn best alone and 28% who need a teacher to learn the best. Sometimes you are given the opportunity to choose how you want to complete a task: alone, with a friend, or in a group. Being aware of your preference can help you choose the social setting that best suits your needs.

Some students may have difficulty learning directly from an adult in a typical classroom setting. They are uncomfortable and usually too tense when under pressure to concentrate in teacher-led situations. For such students, learning either alone or with peers in a group setting or working alone might be a better alternative than working directly with their teachers. You may not always have a choice and sometimes might just need to follow the teacher's plan for the class. However, if your teacher is able to give you a choice, you want to make the right one.

Physiological preferences include time of day and need for intake of snacks. Some students concentrate better in the early or late morning, others do not focus well until afternoon; some are lethargic all day and don't become energetic until night.

You can complete the following questionnaire on time of day by checking the box for TRUE or FALSE after each of the statements, including all the parts of Question 15. If you are not sure, leave the space blank.

CHAPTER 7: Who? When?

STATEMENT	TRUE	FALSE
1. I usually hate to get up in the morning!		
2. I usually am wide awake at night!		
3. I wish I could sleep late each morning!		
4. I stay awake for a long time after I go to bed.		
5. I only feel wide awake after 10:00 A.M.		
6. If I stay up very late at night, I get too sleepy to remember anything.		
7. I usually feel "low" after lunch.		
8. I get up early in the morning to do a task that requires concentration.		
9. When I can, I do most concentration-requiring tasks in the afternoon.		
10. I usually begin the tasks that require the most concentration after dinner.		
11. I could stay up all night!		
12. I wish I didn't have to go to school until noon!		
13. I wish I could stay home during the day and go to school at night.		
14. I like going to school in the morning!		
15. I remember things best when I concentrate on them:		
a. in the morning		
b. at lunchtime		
c. in the afternoon		
d. before dinner		
e. after dinner		
f. later at night		

Dunn, R., & Dunn, K. (1977). *How to Raise Independent and Professionally Successful Daughters*. Englewood Cliffs, NJ: Prentice Hall, Inc., p. 106.

Use the table below to score your time of day preference. The highest score is the time of day when you have your strongest energy levels.

TIME-OF-DAY ENERGY LEVELS							
Early Morning		Late Morning		Afternoon		Evening	
T	F	T	F	T	F	T	F
8	1	5	3	3	7	2	6
14	3	12	8	5	8	4	8
15a	5	15b	9	9	11	5	14
	10		10	12	13	10	
	11		11	15c	14	11	
	12		12	15d		13	
	13		13			15e	
						15f	
___ + ___		___ + ___		___ + ___		___ + ___	
___/10		___/10		___/11		___/11	

Now that you have an idea of when you learn best, take this information to your parents and teachers and discuss it with them. You can't expect your teacher to change the entire schedule for you to always have math in the early afternoon. But maybe on some days or when it is extremely important for you to understand the material, the schedule can be changed. Maybe a teaching assistant or another student can go over the material with you during your best learning time to make sure that it really sticks. Remember that what works best for you may not work best for others; this information is very personal and learning profiles are unique to each person. Sometimes you will have to attend to tasks which are new and difficult when it is not your optimum learning time or space, so you will need to use extra energy and attention to complete them. If you find them too difficult, you might want to revisit them at another time of day, if possible. There are many ways to make a classroom a friendlier learning environment. The key is getting the information about how you learn from the LS:CY, sharing it with your teacher and parents, and then brainstorming together to come up with the best plan for your learning.

8

Putting It All Together

hen you opened this book, you already knew that you had autism. Now that you have read the book, you have a better understanding of how your autism and your learning style preferences come together to make learning easier and more fun for you. You should also have a better understanding of autism and be able to put into words how this makes you different. You inevitably encounter pitfalls or challenges in your day-to-day life because you have autism; however, with understanding comes power. You now have the power and knowledge to advocate for yourself, to respectfully educate your teachers and those around you. You have a better understanding of what your autism might "look like" in the classroom and how it can affect your learning. In addition, you have a better grasp on things you need to consider and think about when you self-advocate.

Everyone is different. Everyone has different learning style preferences, strengths, and challenges they need to consider to succeed in the classroom, and these preferences have now been clearly explained to you through the LS:CY results. Teachers are aware of these differences and try their best to accommodate all learners, but this is not always easy or possible. However, you have another layer to your differences that some teachers may not have come across and are struggling to understand. You, better than anyone else, know what makes you feel happy and successful and, conversely, what can ultimately lead to disaster for you. You should have a better understanding of those quirky little things that you once thought only applied to you and your autism and could in a flash send you into a tailspin. This is not so; all people have preferences when learning. Yours may just be more specific or intense at times. Your new knowledge will help you put those things in perspective, giving you ideas and tips on how to better organize yourself and getting you the best results.

You have also read some practical suggestions and tools for changing your learning patterns or environment so you will become a more comfortable learner. Teachers and parents are your supporters in this challenge. Share this information with them; teach them how to better teach you now that you have learned what might work best for you. Although you may sometimes feel alone and utterly unique, know that the people around you sometimes need a bit of understanding and knowledge to help them help you through those times. Things that are commonplace for you and that you deal with every minute of every day may be things that even the most enlightened adults around you never even considered or thought about. With a little prompting from you, it may not be such a huge leap for them to adjust their thinking to be more in line with yours, enabling you to learn in a more comfortable way and helping to create a positive classroom for all students.

It Takes a Village—Supporting Your Students or Children with Autism as They Discover Their Preferred Learning Style

As you now understand from reading this book, autism and learning styles are both complex topics. Each has its own definition and comes with sets of possibly difficult questions. When reading along with your child or student, remember that this may be the first time the child has considered autism and learning style independently and most likely the first time either of you has thought about how they can relate to each other.

The old saying, "if you have met one person with autism, you have met one person with autism," could not be more apparent in this context. When throwing preferred learning style into the mix, an even more unique profile is created. Students with autism can sometimes feel alienated and uncomfortable in their environment, both physically and emotionally. Possible difficulties with social interactions along with sensory issues can be very real and serve to create what can seem like barriers to learning. A deeper understanding of how a student learns and basic, sometimes small, changes as to where, how, and with whom he learns may be the enabling factors leading to a more successful classroom. Your student with autism may be presented with many challenges which, when understood by the adults around him, may have reasonably easy fixes. When working through this book and its messages with your student or child, remember that this may all be brand new information. The child may not have had any previous exposure to it. When answering questions or discussing concepts, make sure to listen to what the child is saying, as well as what he is not saying. Let the child digest what he learns and encourage open and honest discussions. It may take some time, maybe additional maturity, for your student or child to fully understand how beneficial a structured plan based on identified strengths and weaknesses can be. Remind the child that these are suggestions for successful learning, not mandates. Let the child experiment and try them on for size before making significant changes which may be difficult to reverse if they truly don't work out. Teach the child the art of self-advocacy so she can speak up and share what she now knows about how she learns and make acceptable suggestions for creating an optimum learning environment.

Appendix

Here are some websites and books that may help you learn more about autism or learning styles.

Autism:

www.autismspeaks.org

A leading autism science and advocacy organization. You can find some interesting and useful apps recommended here.

nationalautismassociation.org

Family information on autism.

www.autism-society.org

Helpful resources about autism as well as updates on latest news and ideas.

www.autismweb.com

Information for parents as well as kids with autism.

www.autismhwy.com

Both informative and fun, including fun games.

Learning Styles:

www.learningstyles.net

A website designed to help people from "6 to 106" begin learning and working smarter.

About the Authors

Karen Burke, CSJ, EdD is an Emeritus Professor at Western Connecticut State University (WCSU) in Danbury, Connecticut. She recently completed 10 years as a WCSU Instructional Leadership Doctoral Program Professor, recipient of the 2009 Connecticut State University Trustees Faculty Research Award. She is a former early childhood and middle school educator, and elementary school administrator.

During the past 20 years, Dr. Burke dedicated her time researching the different styles of learning. She was co-creator of the Learning Style: The Clue to You (LS:CY) Assessment which helps determine individual's learning preferences and effects of using instructional strategies responsive to students' learning-style strengths. Her research has extended to conference presentations, professional development programs, and educational outreach in the United States and over 40 other countries in Central America, South America, the Middle East, Africa, and Asia. Although Karen has traveled the globe lecturing on innovative teaching and learning techniques, the most important lessons she has learned are in global awareness and understanding. As globalization changes the way we live, learn, and work; international education becomes important. "As a global citizen, she gets to see how similar we are to all people, how our cares and concerns and worries are all very similar. And the more we realize we are alike, the easier it will be to accept our differences."

These insights and research projects subsequently lead to more than 40 publications in educational journals and edited books.

Diana Friedlander, EdD is an elementary special education teacher in Ridgefield, Connecticut. She is also an adjunct professor at Western Connecticut State University (WCSU), Danbury, Connecticut, where she teaches in the graduate and undergraduate teacher education programs. Dr. Friedlander has taught students with autism for over 40 years in both private and public schools where she has been an advocate for the successful inclusion of students with special needs into the general education classroom. Her research investigated differences and similarities in learning styles of students with autism and their typical peers. A lifelong student, Dr. Friedlander has just begun fencing, something she has always wanted to learn.

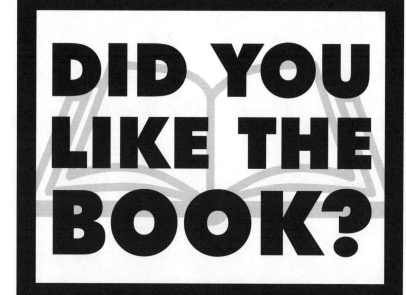